The Power of Prayer
around the World

Lord, teach us to pray . . .

—LUKE 11:1

The Power of Prayer

around the World

GLENN MOSLEY & JOANNA HILL

TEMPLETON FOUNDATION PRESS

PHILADELPHIA & LONDON

Templeton Foundation Press
Five Radnor Corporate Center, Suite 120
100 Matsonford Road
Radnor, Pennsylvania 19087

Library of Congress Cataloging-in-Publication Data
Mosley, Glenn.
    The power of prayer around the world / Glenn Mosley &
Joanna Hill.
        p. cm.
    Includes bibliographical references.
    ISBN 1-890151-47-5 (cloth : alk. paper)
    1. Prayer. 2. Prayers. I. Hill, Joanna. II. Title.
BL560 .M67 2000
248.3'2–dc21   00-064786

Designed and typeset by Helene Krasney
Printed by R. R. Donnelley & Sons
Printed in Mexico

00 01 02 03   04   05   06   10 9 8 7 6 5 4 3 2 1

Contents

Prayer is talking to God and at the same time some inner view of the things that are being prayed for. Answering to this there is something akin to an influx into the perception or thought of the person's mind, which effects a certain opening of his internals towards God. But the experience varies according to the person's state and according to the essence of what he is praying for. If his prayer springs from love and faith, and if he prays about and for heavenly and spiritual things, something like revelation is present within his prayer. This manifests itself in his affection in the form of hope, comfort, or some inward joy.

— EMANUEL SWEDENBORG

Preface

This small book is offered as a gift to all who want to participate in an active, prayerful life. This does not involve changing your lifestyle, although that may eventually happen. It does not involve following any particular discipline, although that might happen, too. You may find that by setting aside time for prayer and gratitude you will be led to develop a spiritual practice that supports growth and positive change. These changes will not come from the outside in, but from the inside out.

We are writing from a Christian viewpoint, in particular from our backgrounds in the Unity Church and Swedenborgian understanding. Our goal, however, is to honor the diversity of ways of prayer and the common humanity of all people who are looking for ways to grow, to become more loving, more wise. In fact, Unity Church itself does not have a conclusive unitary method of prayer, although there are common elements among its various practices.

One of the Unity Church's most nearly universal elements is that the time of prayer is called "the silence." The silence is a frame of awareness entered into for the purpose of putting ourselves in touch with Infinite Wisdom so that our souls may listen to the "still small voice" (I Kings 19:12). Another element is the spirit of thankfulness for answered prayer. Since we may not know going into prayer what is best for us, we are grateful for the answer, whether it is "yes," "no," or "not now." A thankful heart helps to create an open mind to whatever next step of good may be available to us and to those for whom we pray. We include in our praying the health, happiness, abundance, and peace for all humankind.

It is often helpful to begin the silence by reminding ourselves that the Presence that we know as God does not *have* what we need. Rather God *is* what we need. This third common element of Unity prayer serves as a reminder that it is not necessary to inform God of needs during our times of prayer. The Unity Church believes that we are never separate from God and that our time of prayer is either to establish or to re-establish our awareness of that Truth. We pray to know God more fully; we believe God already knows us.

To enter the silence we need to lead ourselves into a tranquil state and ultimately be silent so that we can hear and feel what the Presence would have us know, and therefore do. Since this is an appointment with Holy Spirit, it is important that we be more aware than at any other time. Because physical discomfort can impede awareness, we must take the time to be comfortable. Often this can be achieved by simply repeating the word "relax" or the phrase "relax and let go" until we are truly relaxed. The purpose of this is to present ourselves to God as empty vessels. As the Psalmist wrote, "Be still and know that I am God" (Psalm 46:10). For the Unity Church, such stillness is a truly important step in the silence because we believe stillness is a major pathway to true union with God. Whether we say this Scripture aloud or silently, we must take time to experience stillness, and to return to an awareness of our oneness with God.

When we go into the silence we enter "the secret place of the most High" (Psalm 91:1), a kind of interior closet where we may pray and commune with God. Then we listen so that we may hear what God has to say to us or, as answered prayer is often experienced, to *feel* what guidance God provides. In that peace, we may pray for specific needs and people, but we also pray for the benefit of all humankind. Finally, we express our gratitude to God.

For all the seen and yet unseen blessings You provide and that You are, God, we are grateful. Thank You. Amen.

The Power of Prayer around the World

The fruit of silence is prayer,
The fruit of prayer is faith,
The fruit of faith is love and
The fruit of love is silence.

— MOTHER TERESA

Introduction

Prayer is the universal expression of communication with God, recognized by many cultures for time immeasurable. Whether part of a formal service recited with a congregation of worshipers or an individual, quiet moment, prayer is part of the lives of people from a variety of religions. There seems to be an innate urge among humanity to connect with a higher source of energy and love when we need guidance or direction, and this is called prayer.

Prayer usually involves a petition for some action or favorable outcome of events. It can be thought of as a way to ask for special favors and specific goals, but this type of prayer

How should I pray?
Teach the art of prayer to me,
that I may devote myself to you.
Should I meditate upon
the wonders of your creation?
Should I give thanks for the wisdom
of my elders? Should I praise you
for your many gifts to me?
Should I reflect on all the things
I have done wrong? Or should I simply
wait until you speak to me?
Tell me truly; how should I pray?

—ZOROASTER

may or may not be effective. Prayer also can be a feeling of communion—a shift from selfish preoccupation to love of higher motives and principles. This type of prayer exists when all selfish desire is put aside and we feel ourselves in conjunction with God. At this point, our greatest wish is that God's will be done. There may be pressing concerns that make us turn our sights upward or inward, but we can learn to let go of the end result. Thus, prayer becomes a way of opening up to the universal, loving, creative energy that exists and is far greater than any person could imagine. This is the source of miracles, of faith, and of unconditional love.

Prayer then becomes more than a means to an end; it becomes a state of humility and of awe. It can exist whether we are washing the floor or composing a symphony. It can be an individual experience, a group action, a meditation, an affirmation, or simply a cry for help. Prayer is communion with the Divine, and therefore it can take place throughout the day in the form of a conversation with God. Prayer can be our way

The Answer

When for a purpose I had prayed
and prayed and prayed
Until my words seemed worn and bare
with arduous use,
And I had knocked and asked and
knocked and asked again,
And all my fervor and persistence
brought no hope,
I paused to give my weary brain a rest
and ceased my anxious human cry.
In that still moment,
after self had tried and failed,
There came a glorious vision of God's power,
and, lo, my prayer was answered in that hour.

— LOWELL FILLMORE

of sharing our hopes and wishes, dreams and desires, as well as our fears and needs.

Many people wonder if this process is successful and, if so, what are the principles for greatest effectiveness? There seems to be a universal awareness that in our times of greatest need or greatest joy we call out for help or give thanks. But who are we calling out to? And are we heard?

Emanuel Swedenborg wrote that God already knows what we need, but we must go through the step of asking for it. God hears all prayers and looks only to the heart of the person praying to know the sincerity or appropriateness of the plea. If we want our prayers to be answered, we need to look within ourselves to sense the purity of our heart's request. We can then pray for peace of mind to accept the outcome of our prayer, knowing the end result is not of our doing.

The words we use, the attitude we bring, and the object of our prayers may all play a part in the effectiveness of our worship. As we begin to understand the purpose of prayer, we

Lord, I pray that you may be a lamp
for me in the darkness. Touch my soul
and kindle a fire within it, that it may
burn brightly and give light to my life.
Thus my body may truly become your temple,
lit by your perpetual flame burning
on the altar of my heart. And may the light
within me shine on my brethren
that it may drive away the darkness
of ignorance and sin from them also.
Thus together let us be lights to
the world, manifesting the bright beauty
of your gospel to all around us.

— COLUMBANUS

can see that prayer has within it deep spiritual guidance that will make us wiser and more loving people. Turning to prayer will not only make us better people, but will make the world a better place in which to live.

Thank you, good Lord,
for the gift of belief,
because this has given me
the light of understanding.
It is because I first
believed that you exist that
I can now understand it.

—ANSELM OF CANTERBURY

Prayer, Meditation, and Affirmation

An understanding of the different methods of praying, or conversing with God, can help us to learn the benefits of each and how to utilize the best one at the most opportune time. These techniques have developed within different cultures and some may be easier for certain people, but they are accessible to all. Our advice would be to try several approaches so that they are available to you, depending upon your state of mind and situation.

For example, a three-hour delay at an airport could be an excellent time to try a simple meditation technique. While others are getting anxious and frustrated, we can use the time to

Just as day declines to evening, so often
after some little pleasure my heart declines
into depression. Everything seems dull, every
action feels like a burden. If anyone speaks,
I scarcely listen. If anyone knocks,
I scarcely hear. My heart is as hard as flint.
Then I go out into the field to meditate,
to read the holy Scriptures, and I write down
my deepest thoughts in a letter to you.
And suddenly your grace, dear Jesus,
shatters the darkness with daylight, lifts the
burden, relieves the tension. Soon tears
follow sighs, and heavenly joy floods
over me with the tears.

—AELRED OF RIEVAULX

become calm and more peaceful. We remember one workshop we participated in while attending a very stressful trade meeting that usually left us feeling drained and overstimulated. We were taught how to survive the meeting using a Buddhist walking meditation and simple mantra to quiet the mind and focus our energy, while being totally present with duties at the show. At the end of the meeting, rather than feeling exhausted and drained, we felt invigorated and full of energy. We had learned to turn our attention to a loving, peaceful place rather than dissipate it into the crowds and chaos of forty thousand people.

The key to any of these methods, of course, is learning to access the wisdom we have available to us—to pay attention and remember what we have been taught. If we do not know what to remember, it is time to start looking and reading, and this book is a good first step in our search. As we read the works of holy people, Scripture, the lives of saints and yogis, we will find amazingly similar approaches to wisdom, love, and living good lives of service to our friends, families, and

My God, if I dared to grumble, the only thing of which I would complain is that you have not sent enough good spiritual guides into your Church. There are so many who can put on an outward display of godliness, but inwardly have little real knowledge or holiness. . . . I thank you that you hid the mysteries of your truth from such people, who are so great in their own eyes. Instead you chose to reveal yourself to those who count themselves as nothing. Yet those who have true holiness and true understanding are often so reluctant to serve as spiritual directors, saying that they are not worthy to offer guidance to others. Put into their hearts the courage and the confidence to share with others the grace which they have received.

— FENELON

communities. These approaches can fill us with goodness we can draw from in times of difficulty. They can also help us to control our self obsession and pride in times of great success. If we learn to look first within for guidance, and then acknowledge the source of all good, we can find peace of mind. We can learn to pray—to connect with God for strength when we are in greatest need as well as in gratitude when we are feeling great joy.

Prayer

One type of prayer is the informal, conversational version, as if we were talking to God as our counselor, best friend, or parent. We can use this as a running commentary on life or as a means of seeking a higher wisdom as we work, rest, and recreate. A wise and successful business person we know always starts business meetings with prayer, praying not for good profits but for wise decisions that are good for all concerned. This helps people to focus on the best possible solution for all, not just for themselves.

Hail Mary

Hail Mary, full of grace,
The Lord is with thee.
Blessed are thou amongst women
And blessed is the fruit of thy womb, Jesus.

Holy Mary, mother of God,
Pray for us sinners,
Now and at the hour of our death.
Amen.

Petition is another kind of prayer, one by which we are asking for specific results, such as a better job, the presence of a soul mate, more money, or for the health of ourselves or others. The results of this kind of prayer have varying rewards, ones that often depend upon the actual source of the request. In general, we would expect that pleas made for the healing of a loved one might be more successful than requests to win the lottery. That is, pleas of a loving, spiritual nature might be more likely to be fulfilled than pleas of a selfish, materialistic one.

The third kind of prayer is that which takes place in formal ceremonies, such as in a church, synagogue, or ashram. These usually follow a predictable format from day to day or week to week. These prayers are often based on historical precedent or cultural orientation and can be very comforting because they represent familiar and appreciated traditions. For example, Catholics can turn to the Hail Mary as a centering prayer in times of stress. The familiar words may evoke a

Whether He replies or not, keep calling Him—
Ever calling in the chamber of continuous prayer.
Whether He comes or not,
Believe He is ever approaching nearer to you
With each command of your heart's love.
Whether He answers or not, keep entreating Him.
Even if He makes no reply in the way you expect, ever
know that in some subtle way He will respond.
In the darkness of your deepest prayers,
Know that with you He is playing hide and seek.
And in the midst of His dance of life, disease, and death,
If you keep calling Him, undepressed
by His seeming silence,
You will receive His answer.

—PARAMAHANSA YOGANANDA

feeling of connection with family and hundreds of years of tradition. The shortcoming of this method is that it can become a ritualistic type of worship without real feeling behind the prayers. It is not the prayers, but the participation on the part of the person praying that may determine how effective this form of prayer may be.

MEDITATION

Individual meditation, a quieting of the mind, forms yet another type of prayer. It can involve the use of a mantra or focusing technique and, although it may not be as goal oriented as some of the other forms, it can also be thought of as prayer since it involves communion with God.

There are different methods of meditation. One involves clearing the mind of all thoughts, of going to the place of "no thought." To employ this method, we should find a place to sit quietly without distraction and simply be. This might be the most difficult thing for the Western mind to attempt and for some people it takes years of

I have arrived.
I am home
in the here,
in the now.
I am solid.
I am free.
In the ultimate
I dwell.

—THICH NHAT HANH

practice. In fact, yoga was developed to make the body flexible and peaceful enough that it could sit quietly in meditation. The process of "sitting" as such is generally a Buddhist approach; individuals who want to pursue this method should find a good teacher to act as a guide.

An easier method of meditation is to focus the mind on an object, whether it be a word, mantra, or uplifting concept such as a short quote from Holy Scripture. Again, we need to find a quiet time and space, perhaps sitting on the floor in a cross-legged position or in a comfortable chair. We may meditate with open or closed eyes. If we do not fight distractions as they arise, but simply replace them with the mantra or image we choose, our minds, at some point, will become very peaceful and focused on our object of meditation. As we meditate, we may allow images and colors to appear and simply observe them as we keep our conscious mind occupied with the mantra. We should not become overly distracted by what comes to us; in fact, we may choose to watch our thoughts and feelings from the

Let the words of my mouth and
the meditation of my heart
be acceptable to you,
O Lord, my rock and my redeemer.

— PSALM 19:14

perspective of an observer. When we practice this method we will realize we are more than our thoughts and feelings. A part of us is an observer. That quiet space or Presence, "the still small voice" (I Kings 19:12), is what we are experiencing. As we become more comfortable with our time of meditation, we will find ourselves refreshed and invigorated when we return to our daily routines.

We should not be discouraged if such meditation is difficult at first; let us simply return to the mantra or prayer and relax. We can also use the breath as a meditation. As we observe the breath going in and out, we learn to become one with the breath of life, the source of energy or prana that permeates our cells. As we become one with the universal energy, we leave our cares and worries behind.

Meditation often works best first thing in the morning, before our minds become cluttered with day-to-day worries, or last thing at night before retiring. However, any time we have a few minutes and feel the need to refresh, refocus, and reorient ourselves is a

I would be true for there are those who trust me.
I would be pure for there are those who care.
I would be strong for there is much to suffer.
I would be brave for there is much to dare.
I would be friend of all, the foe, the friendless.
I would be forgiving and then forget the gift.
I would be humble for I know my weakness.
I would look up, and laugh, and love, and live.

— Anonymous

good time. Sometimes when life gets too hectic and stressful, our bodies will go into their own forms of meditation, a purposeful pause, as a way of helping us get perspective on the importance of things. It often happens when we are paying too much attention to the outer world and not enough to the inner one.

AFFIRMATION

Affirmation, or giving thanks, is another method of prayer. It involves a sense of gratitude for having already received that for which we are praying. Jesus illustrated this point when he instructed his disciples in prayer, "Whatever you ask for in prayer, believe that you have received it and it will be yours" (Mark 11:24). The second part of his lesson was just as telling: "whenever you stand praying, forgive, if you have anything against anyone, so that your Father in heaven may also forgive you your trespasses" (11:25). Thus, not only do we pray in gratitude, we pray also in humility for the ability to forgive and be forgiven. We will be blessed to the extent that we are also as generous and loving to others.

Lord, inspire us to read your Scriptures
and meditate upon them day and night.
We beg you to give us real understanding
of what we need, that we in turn
may put its precepts into practice.
Yet we know that understanding
and good intentions are worthless,
unless rooted in your graceful love.
So we ask that the words of Scriptures
may also be not just signs on a page,
but channels of grace into our hearts.

— ORIGEN

This is the principle of affirmation—creating a positive attitude toward life. As we practice being grateful for our families, our work, the beauty of the trees, and innocence of a child, we will develop this sense of gratitude in our daily lives, so that it will not feel foreign to us when we extend it to prayerful affirmations. One of Sir John Templeton's Laws of Life illustrates this principle: "An attitude of gratitude creates blessings."

Let us pray in thanks for acceptance to the college of our choice, for the loving partners with whom we will share our lives, for the safe journeys we are taking. Let us pray positively, for the qualities with which we infuse our request will be the qualities that come back to us. If we cringe in fear from situations or worry about people and relationships, our negative thinking will only increase our own discomfort and that of others. To love others is not to worry about them; it is to surround them with positive, loving energy and ask only for their greatest spiritual good. Whether we are praying at the side of a dying loved one or soothing a child's temper tantrum, we cannot always "make it

In Serious Illness

Lord, you are the only source of health
for the living, and you promise eternal life
to the dying. I entrust myself
to your holy will. If you wish me
to stay longer in this world, I pray that you
will heal me of my present sickness.
If you wish me to leave this world, I readily
lay aside this mortal body, in the sure hope
of receiving an immortal body which shall enjoy
everlasting health. I ask only that you relieve me
of pain, that whether I live or I die, I may rest
peaceful and contented.

— ERASMUS

right." What we can do is bring the highest form of our love to the situation and pray to God for guidance and correct action. "Let the words of my mouth and meditation of my heart be acceptable to you, O Lord, my rock and my redeemer" (Psalm 19:14). That should be our highest prayer.

When we learn different approaches to prayer, we have available various methods to calm our minds and hearts. As we learn to access the quiet space within, we bring the greatest gift we can to any situation—a sense of peace from which real wisdom can flow and genuine love can flourish.

An aspect of prayer that can be overlooked is the possibility that it is not a one-way conversation. As we send out heartfelt requests in the form of prayer, let us also pray for the awareness to recognize guidance when it comes back to us. An openness to receiving answers to our prayers can make us more receptive to the various forms the answers can take.

These answers may come as actual words, pictures, or feelings as we pray. Other times there can be a delay and the

Great Spirit, Great Spirit,
my Grandfather, all over the earth
the faces of living things are all alike.
With tenderness have these come up
out of the ground.
Look upon these faces of children
without number
and with children in their arms,
that they may face the winds
and walk the good road
to the day of quiet.

— BLACK ELK

message can come from the most unexpected places. We know of people who have received answers to prayers from the back of a well placed t-shirt or billboard, a seemingly disconnected comment from a street person, or picking up a book at a garage sale, which happened to a friend of ours. He was praying and searching for a deeper meaning to his life, asking God to guide him in his spiritual path and chanced upon a classic about the afterlife when he was searching for bargain housewares. By simply trusting the process and being aware of seemingly unrelated events, he was receptive to Divine guidance that can come in many forms.

The next prayer should then be for the courage to follow through, to act upon a commitment, which is the prayer. If we can develop the strength to actualize our faith, based on the answers to our deepest wishes, we will grow stronger and more trusting. We will develop a confidence that our prayers are heard and answered.

Irish Prayer

May there always be work
for your hands to do.
May your purse always
hold a coin or two.
May the sun always shine upon
your windowpane.
May a rainbow be certain
to follow each rain.
May the hand of a friend
always be near to you and
May God fill your heart
with gladness to cheer you.

The Use of Prayer
in Various Religions

When we look at how prayer is used in different religious traditions, we notice the striking similarities among the diversity. People come together as a group, whether in Hindu temples or Jewish synagogues. Most engage in prayers of gratitude, of devotion, of petition. Prayer marks the passages of one's life, the seasons of the year, and the hours of the day. With the richness of the religious traditions of our world, we can learn to appreciate the beauty of the many facets of our Creator in the expressions of those who are seeking to open their hearts to God.

Prayer for Yom Kippur

How fragile is life,
How fleeting our days.
From dust we are born to praise You.
When life slips away to dust we will go.
How fragile is life and we praise You.
Like a clay pot when it breaks,
Like a blade of grass withers,
Like a flower fading fast,
A shadow flitting past.
Like a cloud we disappear,
Like the wind we sigh,
Like dust we're blown to distant shores,
Like dreams we are no more.

—ADAPTED BY ESTA CASSWAY

JUDAISM

Jewish prayer is an elaborate set of rituals designed to bond a community and to transmit the experience from generation to generation. The Shema is recited when retiring at night and awakening in the morning. The Amidah is the central part of the three daily services. There are other prayers that distinguish the Sabbath from the rest of the week as well as special prayers for the many seasons, festivals, and holy days, such as Passover and Yom Kippur, which make up the rich tradition of Judaism.

Jewish prayer can encompass praise (the Psalms), petition for healing or forgiveness, gratitude—usually after eating— or powerful emotions that transport the worshiper beyond the words of the prayers themselves. Prayer often takes place in a minyan, which is a quorum with a minimum of ten Jews. The minyan symbolizes the Jewish people, past and present. The prayers are often chanted or sung by a cantor or a non-clergical congregant.

Sim Shalom

Grant us peace,
Your most precious gift.
May it be in our midst, forever.
May You send happiness,
blessings and kindness.
Grant us shalom, for Israel,
and all the world.
Sim shalom.

—ADAPTED BY ESTA CASSWAY

Jewish prayer is both a personal and community experience. It defines the peoplehood and community of Israel and articulates the theological views of the Jews.

CHRISTIANITY

The early basis for Christian prayer comes from the plea of the disciples for Jesus to teach them to pray. In response, Jesus gave them a model prayer for Christians then and now, a prayer that has since become known as the Lord's Prayer. In addition, Jesus warned against hypocrisy and public posturing when praying, and urged his disciples to pray even though God already knew their needs. When the disciples were not able to heal a young man with epilepsy, Jesus stated that this type of healing requires prayer; in other words, assistance from a higher source is necessary in order for miracles to occur.

Early Christians prayed at specific times during the day, following the Jewish pattern of praying. These prayers were

The Lord's Prayer

Our Father who art in heaven
hallowed be thy Name.
Thy kingdom come
Thy will be done
As in heaven so upon the earth.
Give us this day our daily bread
And forgive us our trespasses
As we forgive those
Who trespass against us.
Lead us not into temptation
But deliver us from evil.
For Thine is the kingdom,
the power and glory,
Forever and Ever.
Amen.

collected into a Book of Hours, which was filled also with psalms, hymns, and readings for private use.

In addition to the Lord's Prayer, the Eastern Orthodox used the Jesus prayer, "Lord Jesus Christ, Son of God, have mercy on me a sinner," which was repeated continually to provoke a mystical union with God. The Roman Catholic Church developed the use of the rosary and Hail Mary for devotional praying, as well as prayers associated with specific sacraments, which developed eventually into the Mass. With the Reformation came new ways of worshiping and new liturgies from the Protestant perspective. These and other different interpretations of the religion created worship and prayer of great variety.

Christian worship traditionally takes place within a church where services are held on Sundays. The service usually contains Bible readings, songs, prayers, a sermon, and often Communion. Some denominations follow a strict order of worship; others allow for free expression of prayer during the services. No matter what the specific Christian tradition,

In fact, God is peace.
So when any one of you prays, then say,
"All benedictions are for God;
and so are all prayers and all that is good.
Peace upon you, O God.
Peace upon us, and upon all genuine
servants of God,"
for if you say this, it will reach out
to every true servant of God
in the heavens and the earth;
I testify that there is nothing worthy
of worship
but God and that Muhammad is a
servant and messenger of God.

— MUHAMMAD

prayer remains an integral part of personal and public worship.

ISLAM

Prayer in Islam is one of the five pillars of the religion, which also include the declaration of faith, fasting during Ramadan, charitable donations to be distributed among the needy, and pilgrimage to Mecca.

There are very specific rules set down for Islamic prayer. It is to be practiced five times a day—at dawn, noon, afternoon, sunset, and nighttime. Before praying, one must purify oneself, which involves washing the face, hands, and feet, and cleaning the mouth, nose, and teeth. Prayers are to take place in a clean space, often using a prayer rug. The ritual involves elements of bowing, touching the forehead to the ground, kneeling, and repeating specific prayers for the times of day. These prayers can be shared with a group or alone. Specific prayers also mark special events, such as birth, death, and marriage, and are part of yearly festivals.

O Lord, grant us to love Thee;
grant that we may love those
that love Thee;
grant that we may do the deeds
that win Thy love.

—MUHAMMAD

In addition, on Fridays all Muslim men gather at the mosque for afternoon prayer, although this is not theoretically a holy day. In Islam every day is considered holy and every location is a mosque, since there is no special distinction between the sacred and the ordinary. The practice of Islam can be thought of not just as a religion, but as a way of life with prayer playing a significant part.

HINDUISM

Hinduism is an ancient religion based on the Vedas, which are Sanskit holy texts from India. Some of the beliefs include reincarnation and the desire for release from rebirth, called moksha. The Hindus believe that what passes from one incarnation to the next is the soul, the inmost essence of a person, called Atman. All of the universe is held together with a universal consciousness called Brahman, who is the force behind all the deities and is the creative force of the universe. Hindus believe that Atman is part of Brahman.

With all thy strength fly unto God,
And surrender thyself, and by his
Grace thou shall obtain Supreme Peace
And reach the Eternal Home.

—FROM THE BHAGAVAD GITA

Complete devotion to spiritual practice, however, takes place only after the duties of life, such as raising a family and providing for its material well being, are satisfied. These responsibilities might also be considered religious duties to be fulfilled before a person devotes time to the study of sacred texts and renunciation, or leading the life of a holy person.

A famous Hindu religious writing is the Bhagavad Gita, which is called "The Song of the Lord." It tells the story of a young warrior named Arguna and his charioteer, Krishna, who is really God in disguise. Krishna explains to Arguna the meaning and purpose of life, including his duty to fight and the need to remain unattached to the outcome, thus remaining as calm as a yogi. Much of the Bhagavad Gita can be recited as a prayer, such as, "O Lord of Sleep, I am the Atman seated in the heart of all beings. I am the beginning, I am the middle, I am the end of all beings" (Bhagavad Gita 10:20).

Most worship takes place in Hindu households, which contain domestic shrines with statues of various deities. There are

Shanti

May there be peace in the
higher regions; may there
be peace in the firmament;
may there be peace on earth.
May the waters flow peacefully;
may the herbs and plants
grow peacefully; may all the
divine powers bring unto us peace.
The supreme Lord is peace.
May we all be in peace, and
only peace; and may that peace
come unto each of us.
Shanti! Shanti! Shanti!

—FROM THE VEDAS

also public temples and shrines in the villages in which people gather during the day for prayer. Specific rituals that mark special events, such as birth, death, and marriage, are celebrated in the temples, along with study and other community events.

One path of worship is called bhakti, where love of God is expressed through thought and action focused on constant devotion to God. Bhakti can also take the form of song, prayers, chanting, music, and dancing. Another path is that of karma yoga, the yoga of performing good works with no thought of return. The path of knowledge is called jnana, which is liberation through knowledge and wisdom. These methods involve deep commitment, self knowledge, discipline, and dedication to spiritual liberation. Most of the methods would be followed under the guidance of a guru or teacher, who would provide mantras for meditation and other specific practices for the student. The path of Hinduism is one of nonviolence and a sense of responsibility for the actions of our lives. Prayer or meditation is one of the methods that Hindus use to become closer to God.

Be Your Own Lamps

Hold firm to the truth as a lamp
and a refuge and do not look for refuge
to anything beside yourselves.
A monk becomes his own lamp by continually
looking on his body, feelings, perceptions, moods,
and ideas in such a manner that he conquers
the cravings and depressions of ordinary persons
and is always diligent, self-possessed,
and collected in mind. Whoever among
my monks does this, either now or when
I am dead, if he is anxious to learn,
will reach the summit.

—THE BUDDHA

BUDDHISM

Buddhism developed from Hinduism and contains within it many of the same concepts. Its founder, Siddhartha Gautama, was born into a wealthy Hindu family, but he renounced the pleasures of the world to seek liberation from the endless, meaningless cycle of life.

At first he followed a path of extreme asceticism, gaining discipline and control through fasting and meditation, but not true liberation. Eventually he renounced this austere path and found enlightenment through a method he developed to calm the mind and by avoiding extremes of deprivation or indulgence. Sitting under the bodhi tree, he was able to perceive the true nature of things. He then taught this "Middle Way" to his followers as a way to release themselves from suffering caused by attachment to bodily desires, hungers, wants, and feelings. This teaching is contained within the Four Noble Truths, which deal with the nature of suffering and attachment.

Since pure awareness of nowness
is the real Buddha,
in openness and contentment
I found the Lama in my heart.
When we realize this unending natural mind
is the very nature of the Lama,
then there is no need for attached,
grasping, or seeking prayers or
artificial complaints.
By simply relaxing in this uncontrived,
open, and natural state,
we obtain the blessing of aimless
self-liberation of whatever arises.

— DUDJOM RINPOCHE

The purpose of human existence according to Buddhism is to attain Nirvana. The way to do this is by following the Eightfold Path, which is right views, right thoughts, right speech, right action, right livelihood, right effort, right mindfulness, and right concentration.

From this basic teaching many schools of Buddhism developed and spread from India to China, Tibet, Korea, and Japan. Their holy scriptures, practices, and prayers vary, but there are some similarities. For instance, a Buddhist temple can honor many Buddha incarnations because the original Buddha is not worshiped as a deity, only as a special person who attained a state of enlightenment that all have the capacity to realize. Buddhist devotion usually begins with the acknowledgment of the three refuges: "I take refuge in the Buddha; I take refuge in the Dharma (true path); I take refuge in the Sangha (community)."

Since Buddha reached his liberation through meditation, it is the primary Buddhist practice. Some schools, such as

From the blossoming lotus of devotion,
at the center of my heart,
Rise up, O compassionate master,
my only refuge!
I am plagued by past actions
and turbulent emotions:
To protect me in my misfortune
Remain as the jewel-ornament on the crown
of my head, the mandala
of great bliss,
Arousing all my mindfulness
and awareness, I pray!

—JIKME LINGPA

Tibetan Buddhism, use a mantra as the focus of their meditations; one famous mantra is "Om Manipadme Hum," which means "O, the jewel in the lotus." Repetition of this phrase can create positive karma, or well being in this life or the next. Other schools use an image of a holy person or an object, such as a candle. Another method is to look closely at the thoughts and feelings that arise in meditation.

The Tibetans use prayer flags and prayer wheels with Scripture on them as a way of worship. They hang the flags in temples and special places and believe that the prayers are actualized when the wind blows through them. The prayer wheels are cylinders inscribed with a prayer on the outside and contain a scroll with other mantras on the inside. The rotation of the wheel in worship services activates the forces of the text.

In addition, there are often festivals that take place with special prayers and ceremonies. Some of these festivals celebrate the birth of Buddha, the New Year, and other special events.

Those who know do not say;
those who say do not know.
Close the senses, shut the doors;
blunt the sharpness,
resolve the complications;
harmonize the light,
assimilate to the world.
This is called mysterious sameness.
It cannot be made familiar,
yet cannot be estranged;
it cannot be profited,
yet cannot be harmed;
it cannot be valued,
yet cannot be demeaned.
Therefore it is precious for the world.

— LAO-TZU

Buddhism is a path of compassion and mindfulness, which means being aware of every thought, every action, every feeling, and seeing how they affect others. In order to overcome negative traits, we first must acknowledge them. This practice becomes one of constant consciousness, of paying attention to what is taking place here and now rather than worrying about the past and the future. This attitude could be thought of as a state of prayer.

OTHER RELIGIONS

In the myriad of other religious traditions can be found practices that support prayer as an integral part of worship. Practicers of Taoism, a Chinese religion, seek to align themselves with the Tao—the "way" or natural flow of the universe—in a state of awareness and serenity. The main text of their religion is one of simple, wise teachings that can be meditated upon and used as prayer. Taoists developed yoga and other methods of healing to align the body's energies

Countless are your names, countless
your dwelling-places;
The breadth of your kingdom is beyond
our imagination.
Even to try and imagine your kingdom
is foolish.
Yet through words and through music
We speak your name and sing your
praise.
Words are the only tools we have
to proclaim your greatness,
And music our only means
of echoing your virtue.

—GURU NANAK

with this universal energy, and chose humility and simplicity as a way of life.

Native Americans and other indigenous peoples often use songs, dancing, and drumming in a meditative, prayerful way. The purpose of these ceremonies is to petition certain favors, such as a successful hunt, or to mark the passage of a young person to adulthood.

The Sikh faith, from India, combines prayers from Islam and Hinduism in its worship service. Its founder, Guru Nanak, had an enlightenment experience that showed him God's path, which was neither Hindu nor Muslim, but can be known through the Guru.

The Bahá'í faith is another that honors many faiths, drawing from the Torah, New Testament, and the Qu'ran. However, it also has sacred texts from its own teachers, Bahá'u'lláh and 'Abdu'l-Bahá, which include collections of prayers. The Bahá'í believe in the unity of God and his prophets and the unity of the human race. Their worship involves obligatory prayers each

O God! Refresh and gladden my spirit.
Purify my heart. Illumine my powers.
I lay all my affairs in Thy hand.
Thou art my Guide and my Refuge.
I will no longer be sorrowful and grieved;
I will be a happy and joyful being. O God!
I will no longer be full of anxiety,
nor will I let trouble harass me. I will not
dwell on the unpleasant things of life.
O God! Thou art more friend to me
than I am to myself. I dedicate myself
to Thee, O Lord.

—'ABDU'L-BAHÁ

day. They are in the process of building prayer centers for people of all faiths for collective worship. These centers have nine entrances to honor the nine major religious traditions.

Thus we see that prayer can take many forms—from structured, mandatory participation to solitary meditation. The unifying element is the aspiration of the human soul seeking connection and upliftment. This feeling is felt and expressed around the world through prayer.

If you are in search of the place
of the soul, you are the soul.
If you are in search of a morsel
of bread, you are the bread.
If you know this secret,
then you know
that whatever you seek,
you are that.

— RUMI

Learning to Pray

No matter what religious or spiritual tradition we might follow, there are certain mental, emotional, and physical attitudes that make prayer more effective. We can choose our method; we can choose our religious orientation; and we can also learn to choose correct attitude. This is what will make the difference in whether or not we feel our prayers are heard and answered. Following are some basic factors to consider when praying:

1. Attitude matters. How can we pray for peace for others when we are full of rage? Why pray for forgiveness for what we have done until we have forgiven those who have mistreated

The Great Invocation

From the point of Light within the Mind of God
let light stream forth into the minds of men.
Let light descend on Earth.
From the point of Love within the Heart of God
let love stream forth into the hearts of men.
May Christ return to Earth.
From the center where the Will of God is known
let purpose guide the little wills of men—the purpose
which the masters know and serve.
From the center which we call the race of men
let the plan of Love and Light work out.
And may it seal the door where evil dwells.
Let Light and Love and Power
restore the Plan on Earth.

us? Why pray for healing for ourselves if we continue to do destructive things to our bodies? We must ask ourselves if we are praying from a state of mind that will enable us to be receptive to the gift.

If we cannot pray from this place of peace, or forgiveness, or well being, we can pray to know that space. We can pray for clarity to face our weaknesses and strength to overcome them. Until we get to this state of mind, our prayers, wishes, and desires will reflect our lack of equilibrium. We must find the balance within ourselves and align our positive state with a heartfelt request.

2. Be honest. If our religious tradition or spiritual path includes formal prayers, we should take the time to understand what they are saying. How many of us, for example, have looked closely at the words of the Twenty-third Psalm? Within it are wisdom and assurance and much guidance. Let us be

The Lord is my shepherd, I shall not want.
He makes me lie down in green pastures;
He leads me beside still waters; He restores my soul.
He leads me in right paths for his name's sake.
Even though I walk through the darkest valley
I will fear no evil; for you are with me;
Your rod and your staff —they comfort me.
You prepare a table before me
in the presence of my enemies;
You annoint my head with oil;
my cup overflows.
Surely goodness and mercy shall follow me
All the days of my life,
And I shall dwell in the house
of the Lord my whole life long.

—Psalm 23

sincere about what we are saying and praying in order for our words and thoughts to have power. The more honest and truthful we are in every aspect of our lives, the more clearly and immediately our external world will reflect our inner state. If we are saying one thing and doing something else, we will experience confusion and disconnection between our deepest wishes and their realization. The prayer of our actions rather than our words may be the prayer that is answered.

When we feel victimized and powerless, we must first look at the level of integrity in our lives. Do we deal with issues in the family, at the workplace, even our own feelings with impeccable honesty? Do we allow little white lies, such as "Just tell her I am out of the office," to slip into our excuses? Learning to tell the truth is the first step in any true spiritual path. Until we do that, our words and prayers will be empty and powerless and our lives will feel the same. "The truth shall set you free."

We must therefore pray with honesty. Let us know what words we are saying and let them be the true expression of our

The life that we have asked and obtained
from the creator, this we shall put to good use.
It is ours, He has put us in control of it.
Remember that Earthmaker put the means
of obtaining the goods of life in control
of every single spirit he created. Let us,
therefore, concentrate our minds upon
the creator above. Be assured that he
will not take anything from us
without giving something in return.
That is what he himself said. So, if we pour
a handful of tobacco for him who is
up above, he will indeed take it,
he will not reject it.

— WINNEBAGO MEDICINE SOCIETY

being. If they are not, pray only from our own truth by finding or creating prayers that reflect what is true for each of us. Only then are we building a true foundation for spiritual growth.

3. Pray with feeling. Once we are in a place of calm and are speaking words, or thoughts, of truth, we must next focus on the feelings from the heart, so that we may infuse our prayers with a sense of caring, of emotion. The most beautiful, evocative prayer delivered from a dull, lifeless state is like a beautiful letter delivered to the post office without a stamp. It will not go anywhere.

When we pray, let us concentrate our energy on our hearts. See and feel the words and images going out from our hearts to God. If we are praying to conceive a child, feel the joy in the sensation of holding a newborn. If we are looking for that great new job, feel the fulfillment of an opportunity to express ourselves through useful work. We must infuse our

Lord, I seek you with all my heart,
with all the strength you have given me.
I long to understand that which I believe.
You are my only hope; please listen to me.
Do not let my weariness lessen my desire
to find you, to see your face. You created
me in order to find you; you gave me strength
to seek you. My strength and my weakness
are in your hands: preserve my strength, and
help my weakness. Where you have already
opened the door, let me come in; where
it is shut, open at my knocking. Let me always
remember you, love you, meditate upon you,
and pray to you, until you restore me
to your perfect pattern.

—Augustine of Hippo

wishes and hopes or sense of communion with God with the feelings of love and joy, knowing that is what will propel them.

Another method is to feel the prayer in our hearts and then move it up through the body, up through the throat. When we feel it at the space between and just above our eyes, and then release it through the top of the head, it is as though we are releasing it directly to God. This process will put us in a state of calm awareness and will fill us with much joy.

4. Pray from gratitude. When we are grateful, our hearts are open and receptive. We know that we are being provided for and that what we receive is good. Emanuel Swedenborg, a Swedish theologian, said "For one who walks with the Lord, all that happens, even though it might appear bad, is ultimately for the good." This attitude helps to make us grateful for all that occurs, even though we may not understand it.

Indeed, we can be grateful for what we are praying for, as though we have already received it. If we are angry and upset

Thank You Prayer

Thank you, God, for this wonderful land.
Thank you, God, for caring.
Thank you, God, for your helping hand.
We'll thank you, God, by sharing.
A little bit here, a little bit there,
Growing vegetables, fruit, and wheat,
We'll farm the fields and milk the goats,
There'll be plenty for all to eat.
Thank you, God, for the morning sun.
Thank you, God, for sharing
Your seeds and water, your starlit skies,
We'll thank you, God, by caring.

— ESTA CASSWAY

about a broken relationship, we may pray with gratitude for the solace that we know exists. If a loved one is sick, let us pray with thanks for his or her healing. If others are persecuting us, we may pray with gratitude for peaceful resolution, not for retribution.

The mastery of this step requires a leap of faith. We are no longer sending a purchase order to God with a special request, but sending a thank-you note for an unopened gift. We must learn to be grateful for whatever is inside.

5. Pray now. We must not wait until we are ready, until we have the perfect sanctuary set up for our personal sacred space, until we find the best church or spiritual path. Instead, let us pray for these things now. Let us pray as we walk, as we work, as we create. This will put us in touch with the creative force of the universe and keep us in a state of humility and wonder. It will make us open and receptive to others and help us to wish only for what is best for all concerned. As our

Lord, Lord, you are the Lord.
You created all things.
You are the master of the forest.
You are the master of the animals.
You are our master, and we your servants.
You are the master of life and death.
You rule, we obey.

— KALAHARI BUSHMAN

connection with God becomes a daily, constant occurrence, we will find ourselves wanting less and enjoying more.

6. Recognize our part in the process. If we pray for a certain result, and it, in fact, happens, we need to recognize what role we played in this outcome. We are the messenger. We have written the letter, put it in the envelope, and delivered it to the recipient. We did not determine the result, but through prayer we did make ourselves receptive to the gift.

The calmer, wiser, more truthful, and more loving we are, the more powerful the message. However, the true source of good that results does not come from our egos. We feel as though it does, and this is not a bad feeling. It empowers us to do more good and effect more positive change in our lives and in the world. However, the source of true power is not from our small, personal selves. It is from God.

7. Detach from the end result. This step is very closely related to praying with gratitude, but it goes a step further. When we

Steer the ship of my life, good Lord,
to your quiet harbour, where I can be safe
from the storms of sin and conflict.
Show me the course I should take.
Renew in me the gift of discernment,
so that I can always see the right direction
in which I should go. And give me
the strength and the courage
to choose the right course,
even when the sea is rough and
the waves are high, knowing that
through enduring hardship and danger
in your name we shall find
comfort and peace.

— BASIL OF CAESAREA

pray with gratitude, we are thankful for what we receive and our prayer reflects a sense of fullness, not deprivation.

Next, we let go of the prayer. We send it forth filled with our positive, loving energy. We do not need to test, judge, or evaluate what we have prayed for. We let it go knowing that ultimately, "May God's will be done" is the only prayer. We shift from being the person who is praying to being the prayer and, at that point, we know we are in good hands.

Have your own way, Lord, have your own way,
You are the Potter, I am the clay;
Mould me and make me after your will,
As I am waiting, yielded and still.

—Brother Ramon

Research on Prayer

Because prayer is such a fundamental component of religious traditions, many people have wondered about the benefits of prayer. Can it be tested and how can we know if it works? There are those who think that empirical research cannot be conducted on matters of faith and there has been little support for this type of research in the past. Another difficulty involves the setting up of objective models to test the results of prayer.

One study in 1988 conducted by R. C. Byrd tested the therapeutic effect of intercessory prayer on heart patients in San Francisco. Half of the almost four hundred patients were randomly selected to be prayed for daily by Christian volunteers.

In your mercy renew to me
all that I need to know,
in order to find peace and joy.
Tell me the truths that are necessary
for the world in which I live.
Show me how I can meditate upon you,
learning from you the wisdom
that I need. I am never tired
of hearing you, because
your words bring life.

—FROM THE BHAGAVAD GITA

These patients were studied for more than ten months and then their cases were analyzed in twenty-six categories, such as the need for antibiotics while in treatment; the occurrence of pulmonary edema; the need for intubation (use of a breathing tube); and other measures of health benefits. The research concluded that in twenty-one of the twenty-six categories, the patients who were recipients of prayer fared much better. For all patients, prayer was used in addition to standard medical care.

Medical schools are beginning to acknowledge the role played by prayer and spirituality in the healing process. There has been a rapid increase in medical school courses that help students learn to understand and utilize a patient's religion during treatment. This number has increased from three in 1993 to at least thirty in 1997, to seventy-two in 2000.

A recent study conducted by Harold Koenig at Duke University Medical Center recently announced the findings that elderly patients who pray regularly are healthier and happier than those who do not. They found that prayer and

O Saviour of the world, teach us how to pray
for those who are lost in desolations of darkness
without the knowledge of the mercy that is yourself.
Give us penitence for the evil in ourselves which has
added to the darkness of the world, and if there be
any small thing we can do to lighten any misery,
show us what it is and help us to do it. Teach us
how to pray with the compassion which is not afraid
to suffer with those who suffer and, if need be,
to enter into darkness with them.

—ELIZABETH GOUDGE

meditation reduce stress and thus can dampen the body's production of damaging stress hormones such as adrenaline. A drop in stress hormones has been linked to a number of health benefits, including a stronger immune response, which can help fight off disease.

For more than thirty years laboratories at the Harvard Medical School have systematically studied the benefits of mind/body interactions. The research established that when a person engages in a repetitive prayer, word, sound, or phrase and when intrusive thoughts are passively disregarded, a specific set of physiological changes ensues. There is decreased metabolism, heart rate, rate of breathing, and distinctive slower brain waves. These changes are the opposite of those induced by stress and have been labeled the relaxation response.

The efficacy of prayer can be tested and confirmed. For those who pray, it becomes clear that prayer benefits not just the person being prayed for, but also the person praying.

Give me, dear Lord, a pure heart
and a wise mind, that I may
carry out my work according to your will.
Save me from all false desires, from pride,
greed, envy and anger, and let me
accept joyfully every task you set before me.
Let me seek to serve the poor, the sad and those
unable to work. Help me to discern honestly
my own gifts that I may do the things
of which I am capable, and happily
and humbly leave the rest to others.
Above all, remind me constantly that
I have nothing except what you give me,
and can do nothing except
what you enable me to do.

— JACOB BOEHME

Conclusion

A woman had a daughter who had received a beautiful garnet cross for her birthday. It was really quite lovely and expensive and a bit too much of a responsibility for the ten-year-old girl to wear on a daily basis. The woman was drawn to it and, with her daughter's permission, began wearing the cross. It radiated a special beauty that came from its precious jewels as well as its religious significance. Once day the girl realized how attached her mother was becoming to the cross and asked that it be returned to her.

Lord and Master, teach me
to surrender totally to thee,
To let go and give myself completely,
To abandon all petty self-centered concerns
And dissolve my illusory sense of separateness
in the great sea of your omnipresence,
To ignite my life as a lamp
to illumine the world
With that ever-shining light
And to serve you by serving one and all—
And, by constantly remembering
and following thy example,
Let my life reflect thy wisdom
all day long.

—LAMA SURYA DAS

There was no way to refuse the request, so the cross then become the daughter's constant companion. One night, the mother had a dream. In the dream she was longing for the cross that had such inner and outer beauty. A voice came from the distance and said, "I will show you how to make a cross for the new church." Using a finger, the unidentified voice in the dream pushed the left hand arm of the cross down to the bottom of the main stem, so that it formed a backward "L." The corresponding right hand arm was slanted up at a forty-five degree angle, so that the entire figure looked like a person in prayer. The voice then said, "This is the new cross."

Perhaps now is the time to take up the new cross, the symbol of prayer. This is not a call for martyrdom or unnecessary sacrifice. It is a call for communion with the Divine. When we feel weak and powerless, we call out for help. From that feeling, we can pray to move to a state of faith in a loving wisdom and creative force that is God. At that point, we are no longer

There are men who hate me;
Let me love them.
There are men I have wronged;
Let them forgive me.

—FROM THE DINKA TRIBE

crying alone in the wilderness, but are sheltered and led to live good lives—lives that are not ruled by selfish desires, but by the search for goodness and truth.

This image of the cross has a deeper meaning. During the Crucifixion, according to the Gospels, Jesus first called out for help, "Oh God, why have you forsaken me?" His very human side was in pain and sadness. Then something happened. At the end, before his human body died, Jesus began to pray for his persecutors, saying "Forgive them for they know not what they do." He then called out, "Father, into your hands I commend my spirit," and with that his body died.

No matter what religion we are born into or which, if any, we choose to follow, there is deep meaning in this transition—from a call for help to love for others, from helplessness to compassionate power. This new cross is not one of suffering; it is one of deep connection. When we join our hearts and minds with the wish to know and do the will of God, we are in prayer. Turning to prayer provides us with the means to

I would go near thee — but I cannot press
Into thy presence — it helps not to presume.
Thy doors are deeds.

— George MacDonald

change our lives and our worlds if we but open up to the possibility.

> *Ask and it will be given to you; seek, and you will find; knock, and it will be opened to you. For everyone who asks, receives, and one who seeks finds, and to one who knocks it will be opened (Luke 11: 9–10).*

You have made for us this law:
that the effect of what comes to us from
without should depend on what we are like within.
Thus no external misfortune will overcome us
if we restrain the vices inside us.
No public disgrace will overwhelm us
if we resist our own disgraceful desires.
No outward disturbance will daunt us if
our intentions are pure. No enemy can rob us
of our peace if our hearts are fixed on you.
No one can do more harm to us than
we do to ourselves; and as soon as
we master ourselves, everything else loses
its power to hurt us. For this spiritual law,
we give you thanks.

—THE LEONINE SACRAMENTARY

Bibliography

Asplundh, Kurt Horigan, ed. *Learning to Pray: Prayers from the Word for Personal Use.* Bryn Athyn, PA: General Church Publication Committee, 1999.

Braden, Gregg. *The Isaiah Effect: Decoding the Lost Science of Prayer and Prophecy.* New York: Harmony Books, 2000.

Bowker, John. *World Religions.* London: Dorling Kindersley, 1997.

Breuilly, Elizabeth, Joanne O'Brien, and Martin Palmer. *Religions of the World: The Illustrated Guide to Origins, Beliefs, Traditions, and Festivals.* New York: Facts on File, 1997.

Chamberlain, Theodore and Christopher Hall. *Realized Religion: Essays on the Relationship between Religion and Health.* Philadelphia: Templeton Foundation Press, 2000.

Crim, Keith, ed. *The Perennial Dictionary of World Religions*. San Francisco: HarperSanFrancisco, 1989.

Dossey, Larry. *Prayer Is Good Medicine: How to Reap the Healing Benefits of Prayer.* San Francisco: HarperSanFranciso, 1996.

Flach, Frederic. *Faith, Healing, and Miracles*. New York: Hatherleigh Press, 2000.

Jafolla, Richard and Mary Alice Jafolla. *The Quest for Prayer: Coming Home to Spirit*. Unity Village, MO: Unity House Press, 1999.

Meeks, Wayne A., ed. *HarperCollins Study Bible*. New York: HarperCollins, 1989.

Smith, Huston. *The World's Religions*. San Francisco: HarperSanFranciso, 1991.

Swedenborg, Emanuel. *Arcana Coelestia,* Volume 3. Translated by John Clowes. West Chester, PA: Swedenborg Foundation, 1998.

Templeton, John Marks, ed. *Worldwide Laws of Life: 200 Eternal Spiritual Principles*. Philadelphia: Templeton Foundation Press, 1997.

————, *Worldwide Worship: Prayers, Songs, and Poetry*. Philadelphia: Templeton Foundation Press, 2000.

White, Philip, ed. *Unity Magazine*. Unity Village, MO: Unity Magazine, May 2000.

Acknowledgments

"Prayer for Spiritual Qualities," from Bahá'í Prayers 1954 © 1996 by the National Spiritual Assembly of the Bahá'ís of the United States. Reprinted with permission of the publisher, the Bahá'í Publishing Trust, Wilmette, IL.

"Those Who Know Do Not Say," from *The Essential Tao: An Initiation into the Heart of Taoism through the Authentic* Tao Te Ching *and the Inner Teachings of* Chuang Tzu. Translated and presented by Thomas Cleary. Reprinted with permission of HarperCollins Publishers, Inc.

From *Rending the Veil: Literal and Poetic Translations of Rumi* by Shahram T. Shiva. (Prescott, AZ: Holm Press, 1995). Used by permission.

"I Have Arrived," from Thich Nhat Hanh, *The Long Road Turns to Joy: A Guide to Walking Meditation* (Berkeley, CA: Parallax Press, 1996). Used by permission.